Knowing (

BOF

Knowing God's Will

Learning to Recognize God's Voice

BOB GASS

Knowing God's Will
Learning to Recognize God's Voice

ISBN 978-0-88270-617-7

Foreword

Bob Gass has once again dug deep into his 50 years of walking with God and clearly outlined the practical steps each of us needs to take in learning to "Know God's Voice!"

Rather than theological "head knowledge" or 3 easy steps to listen to God—the content of this book has been born out of years of personal experience, trusting God and His word and seeing the answers come though, time and time again.

I found this book inspiring and great to read; finding assurance and knowing that God is ever present and ready to lead us as we seek His face and listen to His voice.

I'm sure you will also be encouraged as you learn some practical steps from reading this book.

Ian Mackie
Chief Executive
UCB UK

Contents

1 Hearing God 1

2 Test It! 6

3 What's in Your Bag? 9

4 3 All-Important Principles 20

5 It Takes Time 27

6 Things to Remember
   When God Speaks 35

7 Not Knowing 41

8 What Have We Learned? 51

9 Think Outside the Box 52

10 Be Persistent 55

11 Be Humble 59

12 Do It Now! 65

13 Eliminate Hurry 68

14 Focus on Your Strengths 71

15 Live in God's Presence 76

Acknowledgments 80

CHAPTER ONE

Hearing God

Let's get one thing clear at the beginning of this book: God has a unique, detailed plan for your life and He will reveal it to you step by step. Will it be quick or easy? No, some days it will feel like you're stuck in neutral, or worse, going in reverse. Everybody has those days, even those you admire who seem to "have it all together." They may not tell you about them, but after fifty years of walking with God, I can tell you we all have them.

This book is not the "be all and end all" when it comes to recognizing God's voice. Actually, it's a follow-up to the first book I wrote on the subject: *Guidance for Today: How to be led by God*. It's also a response to many of the readers of our daily devotional, *The Word for You Today,* who keep asking for help when it comes to knowing God's will.

So let's begin by saying—you already have the ability to hear from God and to succeed at whatever He has called you to do!

> *"He has created us...so we can do the good things he planned for us long ago"* (Ephesians 2:10 NLT).

> *"Everything that goes into a life of pleasing God has been miraculously given to us"* (2 Peter 1:3 TM).

> *"It is God who works in you to will and to act according to his good purpose"* (Philippians 2:13 NIV).

> *"We serve...under [obedience to the promptings] of the Spirit"* (Romans 7:6 AMP).

These Scriptures clearly teach that *you* are capable of recognizing God's voice and following

His plan for your life.

Too many of us think of prayer as just talking to God, rarely stopping to wonder if He might want to talk to us. "How does God speak to us?" you ask:

(1) Through His Word. A particular Scripture jumps off the page and takes on a new and more personal meaning. *(2) Through people.* But you can't be so preoccupied, or selective, that you don't recognize or receive them when God sends them into your life to counsel, challenge, encourage or advise you. *(3) Through His Spirit.* The Holy Spirit who lives within us comforts, corrects, guides and stretches us.

The trouble is, many of us don't seem to expect God to speak to us at all. By our actions you'd think that Jesus packed up and went back to heaven forty days after His resurrection and hasn't been heard from since. No, the Bible is full of accounts of God speaking directly to people like us.

If the essence of Christianity is a personal relationship with God, then God must *still* speak today.

But you can't build a relationship on one-way speeches; you need regular, intimate contact between two persons, both of whom speak and both of whom listen. Hearing God speak to us through His Spirit is not only normal, it's essential. Paul wrote, "You...are controlled...by the Spirit, if the Spirit of God lives in you" (Romans 8:9 NIV).

Once you turn your life over to Jesus it can't be business as usual. Your life no longer consists only of that which can be seen, felt or figured out. It calls for walking by faith, trusting God, constantly opening yourself to His voice and to the leadings of His Spirit.

Some of us are reluctant to open ourselves to God's leadings because we know people who claim to be doing this, but their approach scares us. These people seem to have performed a kind of intellectual lobotomy on themselves; now they expect God to choose what they wear to work in the morning and what they eat for dinner at night. They claim to experience a leading an hour, a vision a day, a miracle a week. In reaction to this some of us run in the opposite direction. To us the Spirit's "promptings" seem to go against human nature and conventional thought. Accustomed to steering our own ship, we're squeamish about letting Him lead. We wish the package was a little neater; it seems too elusive and mysterious. It unnerves us. So when we sense the Spirit's leading we analyze it, discuss it and decide it isn't logical; therefore, we don't pay attention to it. What a loss!

Some of us want to obey God's Spirit but we're not sure we know He's really speaking to us: "Am I hearing my own thoughts and desires, or God's voice?" Not wanting to go off the deep end, we avoid the water altogether. All these reactions are understandable. Yet Paul writes, "Since we live by the Spirit, let us keep in step with the Spirit" (Galatians 5:25 NIV). When you open yourself to God's Spirit and stay in step with Him, your life becomes exciting, rewarding, and best of all— fruitful.

CHAPTER TWO

Test It!

G od's leadings are always consistent with His Word. He will never lead you to be unfaithful to your marriage partner, cheat on an examination, exaggerate to a customer, cause strife in a church, spread hurtful gossip, deceive your parents or your children, or do anything else forbidden by Scripture.

Furthermore, His leadings will always be consistent with the person He created you to be. For example: If you love math and are naturally gifted with computers, why would you assume God would call you into music or theology? Or if you don't come alive unless you're in the great outdoors, why do you think He'd lead you to a downtown

9 to 5 office job? Or if you're not comfortable around children, why would He call you to become a schoolteacher? God's leadings don't contradict who He made you to be. He doesn't create you with particular gifts, then expect you to excel at something totally unrelated.

If you sense a leading that seems contrary to what God made you to be, test it carefully. Is God asking you to do this because at present there's no one else to do it? Is He stretching you into new areas so that your faith will grow? Or is this not "a God idea" at all, but rather a distraction from the assignment He's already given you?

Paul told the Ephesian elders about one of his leadings: "Compelled by the Spirit, I am going to Jerusalem, not knowing what will happen to me there. I only know that in every city the Holy Spirit warns me that prison and hardships are facing me" (Acts 20:22-23 NIV). Now, Paul wasn't being asked to do something contrary to his gifts—all the way to Jerusalem he'd be preaching and strengthening the new churches. He was, however, being asked to sacrifice his own safety and comfort in order to reach and bless others.

Not every leading will involve pain and sacrifice, but some will mean gut-wrenching decisions that require you to choose between being comfortable and building godly character; amassing things and seeking first His Kingdom; promoting yourself and serving others.

When it comes to being led by God, here are a few caution lights you should observe: (a) If it requires you to make a major, life-changing decision in a very short period of time. (b) If it requires you to go deeply into debt or place someone else in a position of awkwardness, compromise or danger. (c) If it requires you to shatter family ties or covenant relationships. (d) If it creates unrest in the spirit of mature friends and counselors.

But let's not be afraid. God wants us to test things, not fear or avoid them. He also wants us to step out in faith and follow Him.

CHAPTER THREE

What's in Your Bag?

Larry Walters was a truck driver but his lifelong dream was to fly, so he joined the Air Force in hopes of becoming a pilot. Unfortunately, poor eyesight disqualified him. Then one day Larry got an idea. He went down to the local Army-Navy surplus store where he bought a tank of helium and 45 heavy-duty weather balloons. Back in his yard, Larry strapped the balloons to his lawn chair. Then he packed some sandwiches and drinks and loaded a BB gun, figuring he could pop a few of those balloons when it was time to return to earth.

But when Larry cut the cord he didn't float lazily up; he shot up as if fired from a cannon! Nor did he go up a couple of hundred feet. No, he climbed and climbed until he finally leveled off at eleven thousand feet! So he stayed up there, sailing around for fourteen hours, totally at a loss as to how to get down.

Eventually he drifted into the approach corridor of Los Angeles International Airport. A commercial pilot radioed the tower about passing a guy in a lawn chair, with a gun on his lap, at eleven thousand feet. (Now there's a conversation you'd probably have given anything to have heard!) LAX is right on the ocean, and at nightfall the winds on the coast begin to change.

As dusk fell, Larry began drifting out to sea. At that point the Coast Guard dispatched a helicopter to rescue him. Eventually they were able to hover over him and drop a line with which they gradually hauled him back to earth. As soon as he landed he was arrested. As he was being led away in handcuffs, a reporter called out, "Mr. Walters, why'd you do it?" Larry stopped, eyed him, then replied nonchalantly, "A man can't just sit around!"

You can't just sit around! One day you're going to stand before God to be audited and rewarded for what you did with your life. So it's crucial that you find God's will and give yourself fully to it. If you do, there's no telling how high you'll go.

There are no uncalled human beings. You have a purpose. You have a design. God made you with certain capabilities and this world needs you to use them.

If you watch people who are fulfilling their callings, their motivation level is high. When obstacles come they have amazing endurance to overcome them. They're growing and learning. There's joy in what they do. To miss out on your calling is to miss out on the reason God made you. Whether your job is in a church, at home, or in the world of business, you were created by God, gifted and called by God—and you'd better take your calling seriously! Here are some questions to help you find your life's calling:

(1) What's my raw material? God has given

you a certain personality, temperament and talents, and you have to honor the raw material you've been given. That means asking yourself, "What sort of things do other people tell me I do well? What unlocks my compassion? What angers me?" Sometimes the problem that infuriates you most is the one you've been called to solve.

(2) *What brings me joy?* It's no accident that you enjoy certain activities. Mother Teresa could sing in the midst of India's slums and suffering. Once she attended a gathering of kings and statesmen with their crowns, jewels and silks. She wore a simple sari held together by a safety pin. One world leader asked her if she became discouraged because she saw so few successes in her ministry to the poor, compared to the size of the need. She answered, "No, I do not. God has not called me to a ministry of success; He's called me to a ministry of mercy."

(3) *Why do I do this?* There's a world of difference between loving to do certain things for their

own sake because you were born to love them, and wanting a job because of the financial rewards that flow out of it. There's also a big difference between doing something because God calls you to it, and just doing what your parents, your friends or your ego want.

(4) What are my limitations? Knowing what you're called to do involves discovering what you're *not* good at, and have *not* been called to do. Sometimes we want things because they look good in the lives of others. But if you're not called to it, what blesses somebody else may bury you. If you can acknowledge and embrace your limitations you're well on your way to understanding your calling.

(5) What has God called me to do? You have a calling. It has to do with what God hard-wired into you. You must seek it with an open mind. When people pretend to be something they're not, they live with a chronic sense of inadequacy. They also set themselves up for a lifetime of frustration. So be ruthlessly open to the truth about yourself.

Your calling is something God decides and you discover. "Don't live carelessly, unthinkingly. Make sure you understand what the Master wants" (Ephesians 5:17 TM).

Have you ever mistakenly picked somebody else's luggage off a conveyor belt at the airport and taken it home? Two seconds after opening it you discover the truth—you can't live out of somebody else's bag! You can't wear their clothes or fit into their shoes.

So why do we try to? Parents! Dad says, "Son, your granddad was a farmer, I'm a farmer, and some day you'll inherit the farm." Teachers! A well-meaning teacher warns a young girl who wants to be a stay-at-home mom, "Don't squander your skills. With your gifts you could make it to the top." Church leaders! The pulpit thunders, "Jesus was a missionary. Do you want to please Him? Spend your life on foreign soil." Sound counsel or poor advice? That depends on what God packed in your bag. What if God created the farmer's son with a talent for law, literature, science, or medicine? What if God gave that girl a passion for kids and home-making? If foreign cultures frustrate you while predictability invigorates you, what are the chances that you'd be a happy missionary?

Actually, you'd only contribute to these mind-numbing statistics: (a) Unhappiness on the job affects one-fourth of today's work force. (b) Seven out of ten people are neither motivated nor competent to perform the basics of their job. (c) Fully seventy percent of us go to work without much enthusiasm or passion.

Do you think that glorifies God? What's the cure? God's prescription begins with unpacking your bags: "All the days ordained for me were written in your book before one of them came to be" (Psalm 139:16 NIV). God gives us eyes for organization, ears for music, hearts that beat for justice, minds that understand physics, hands that love care-giving, and legs that run and win races.

Secular thinking doesn't buy this. It sees no

author behind the book, no architect behind the building, and no purpose behind or beyond this life. It says, "You can be anything you want to be." Maybe you can, but the real question is, will you please God or fulfill His plan for your life? Check your bags! "Make a careful exploration of who you are and the work you have been given, and then sink yourself into that" (Galatians 6:4 TM).

Da Vinci painted only one Mona Lisa. Beethoven composed only one Fifth Symphony. And God made only one version of you. He custom-designed you for a one-of-a-kind assignment.

"How can I discover mine?" you ask. Your ability is a key to understanding your destiny! "If anyone ministers, let him do it as with the ability which God supplies" (1 Peter 4:11 NKJV). When God gives you an assignment He gives you certain abilities. To discover your assignment, study your abilities. Your ease with numbers. Your love of computers. Your gift for interior design. Others stare at blueprints and yawn; you read them and say, "I was made for this." Heed the music within. No one else hears it the way you do. Look back. What have you done consistently well? What have you loved to do? Stand at the intersection of your desires and your successes and you'll find your uniqueness.

"The Spirit has given each of us a special way of serving others" (1 Corinthians 12:7 CEV). Away with this deprecating "I can't do anything" and its arrogant opposite "I have to do every-thing." No, you don't! Paul said, "Our goal is to stay within the boundaries of God's plan for us." Don't worry about skills you don't have, and don't covet strengths others do. Just recognize your gifts, then "Kindle afresh the gift of God which is in you" (2 Timothy 1:6 NAS). If you're not sure what God has called you to do, ask Him. He'll reveal it to you.

Furthermore, He will confirm His will for you, through others. In Acts, chapter 13, we read, "The congregation in Antioch was blessed with a number of prophet-preachers…One day as…they waited for guidance—the Holy Spirit spoke: 'Take Barnabas and Saul [later known as Paul] and commission them for the work I have called them to do.' So…they laid hands on their heads and sent them off" (Acts 13:1-3 TM). Now, notice the following things:

(1) God called Paul and Barnabas by name. God knows your name and where you live. Whether you're hiding in a cave like Gideon or out fishing like Peter, the Lord knows where to find you. He doesn't play hide-and-seek with His purpose for your life.

(2) Their calling was confirmed by trustworthy leadership. Those who laid hands on Paul and Barnabas, confirming their calling, were leaders who took time to pray, fast and seek God's will. Such people are a gift. They won't tell you what you want to hear; they'll tell you what you need to hear. They'll cover you, counsel you, correct you and confirm God's direction for your life. Do you have such

people in your life? If not, you're in a vulnerable place. Begin praying and looking for some!

(3) They found their calling in church. Why is this important? Because God gave us the "pastor-teacher to train [us for service], working within Christ's body, the church" (Ephesians 4:11-12 TM). The Holy Spirit still speaks to us today through spiritual leadership as we gather to pray, worship and hear God's Word. One of the reasons many of us lose our way, is because we aren't in the place where God can speak to us objectively through His Word, and subjectively through His Spirit.

CHAPTER FOUR

3 All-Important Principles

When it comes to understanding and fulfilling your God-given assignment, here are three all-important principles:

(1) Learn to take risks. "To one he gave five talents, to another two, and to another one" (Matthew 25:15 NKJV). In Jesus' story, the first two servants "went and traded." They pondered their options, crunched the numbers, took the plunge and dared to fail. And when they succeeded their Master said, "Well done, good and faithful servant" (Matthew 25:21 NKJV). Taking risks in obedience to faith is what separates dreamers from doers. You must be willing to take risks— not foolish risks, but prayed-over, well-considered,

wisely-counseled risks. The biggest mistake—is not to risk making a mistake.

And how about the third servant? He said, "I was afraid, and went and hid your talent in the ground" (Matthew 25:25 NKJV). The first two invested theirs; he buried his. The first two went out on a limb; he hugged the trunk. He made the most tragic and common mistake of giftedness: he failed to benefit his Master with his talent. Some invest their talents and give God credit, others misuse them and give Him grief. Some honor Him with the fruit, others insult Him with excuses. And how did the Master feel about it? "Get rid of this 'play-it-safe' who won't go out on a limb" (Matthew 25:30 TM). Those are words you never want to hear!

Fear is the enemy of faith. And "Without faith it is impossible to please God" (Hebrews 11:6 NIV). So step out in faith; God won't let you down. Take a risk; He won't let you fail. Even if you stumble several times on your way to success, God invites you to dream of the day when you'll feel His hand on your shoulder and hear Him saying, "Well done, good and faithful servant!"

If you're afraid of risking and failing, take a moment and read these familiar but timeless words by Margaret Fishback Powers:

"One night I dreamed I was walking along the beach with the Lord. Across the sky flashed scenes from my life. For each scene I noticed two sets of footprints in the sand. One belonged to me and the other to the Lord. When the last scene of my life flashed before me, I looked back at the footprints in the sand. I noticed that many times along the path there was only one set of footprints. I also noticed that it happened at the lowest times in my life. This really bothered me and I questioned the Lord about it. 'Lord, you said once I decided to follow you that you would walk with me all the way. But I noticed that during the worst times of my life there was only one set of footprints. I don't understand why when I needed you most, you should leave me.' The Lord replied, 'My child, I love you and would never leave you during your times of trial and suffering. When you saw only one set of footprints, they were mine. *It was then that I carried you!'*"

Do you need reassurance? "The Lord, he it is that doth go before thee; he will be with thee, he will not fail thee, neither forsake thee: fear not" (Deuteronomy 31:8). Need more reassurance? "For he hath said, I will never leave thee, nor forsake thee. So that we may boldly say, The Lord is my helper, and I will not fear what man shall do unto me" (Hebrews 13:5-6).

Go ahead, step out in faith. God is with you!

(2) Look for additional streams. "A river went out of Eden to water the garden...and became ...four [streams]" (Genesis 2:10). The vision God has given you may need to be funded by more than one source. God gave Adam four streams of provision, and you are no different. Before your feet hit this planet God had placed dreams, gifts,

talents and destiny within you. All of these came from Him, so surely He will enable you to put them to work. But that may mean having several streams of revenue.

Paul writes, "I know how to live on almost nothing or with everything" (Philippians 4:12 TLB). Sometimes Paul was well supported by the churches; other times he used his skill-set as a tent maker to fund his ministry. Perhaps you're realizing that there's another gift surfacing in your life. If so, embrace it, develop it, use it and watch God make it flourish!

Don't let people label or compartmentalize you; you're not *just* a schoolteacher. You may teach, but also have a gift for money management and be able to counsel those who struggle with budgeting and investment. You may be a factory worker, but also be handy enough to build furniture or fix cars. So create a side business. There's so much you can do to make your talents work for you. Begin to pray, "Lord, I know there's more, show me the extra streams of supply You have entrusted to me that I might be a blessing to You and others."

(3) While you're waiting, invest in the lives of others. God told His ancient people, "I know the plans I have for you...plans to prosper you...plans to give you hope and a future" (Jeremiah 29:11 NIV).

But hope needs a nurturing environment. God didn't give His people permission to take that hope, then just sit back and do nothing. No, He told them exactly what He wanted them to do while He was working out some of the details of their future: "Build houses and settle down; plant gardens and eat what they produce...Also, seek the peace and prosperity of the city to which I have carried you... Pray to the Lord for it, because if it prospers, you too will prosper" (Jeremiah 29:5-7 NIV). While you're waiting for God to turn things around for you, seize the moment and begin investing in the lives of others.

Many of us think we can just do nothing while we wait for God to work, when in reality there's plenty around for us to do. God said, "Invest in those around you, because when they prosper you will too." Many of us don't understand this. We've become concerned about one person only—ourselves. When we mess up, the only person we tend to see is ourselves. But God says, "While you're waiting for Me to do something good for you, begin doing something good for others." That's what Paul meant when he said, "It is more blessed to give than to receive" (Acts 20:35 NAS). Then he added, "The Lord will reward everyone for whatever good he does" (Ephesians 6:8 NIV).

By blessing others you literally open up a channel for God to come through when He blesses you!

CHAPTER FIVE

It Takes Time

God will use other people to speak to us. I received "a word" from one such individual and it proved to be true—dramatically true! It was when I married Debby. At the end of the ceremony the pastor prayed over us, then he looked at me and said, "You are going to reach more people through your writing than you have in all the years of your preaching."

Now, that's a specific and clear word!

At this particular time I was traveling and speaking in different churches, not to mention being scheduled for the next two years. So I had no interest in becoming a writer. Nor was I trained to be one. My schooling finished at fifteen, back home in

Belfast, Northern Ireland. So I confess that I didn't think much about what I was hearing. Plus, it was my wedding day and my mind was on other things.

But Debby was paying attention. Like Mary, who "kept all these things, and pondered them in her heart" (Luke 2:19) she wrote it down, dated it, waited for God to fulfill it, then reminded me of it when it came to pass.

Four years later I wrote my first edition of the daily devotional *The Word For Today*, and gave it to a group of Christian radio pioneers in England called United Christian Broadcasters. That first edition was 3,000 copies. Truthfully, I had no idea what was birthed that day, or how God would cause it to grow. Today we publish millions of devotionals each quarter, in many different languages. So that "word" certainly came to pass.

When people ask me, "Why *you*, Bob? And why at *that* particular time in your life?" I don't have a complete answer, but I will share with you what I know:

(1) I waited almost forty years before writing my first devotional. God took eighty years to prepare Moses for a ministry that would last forty years. That's a two-to-one ratio of preparation to execution! His first forty years were spent in the palace learning the secrets and ways of Egypt. His second forty were spent in the wilderness learning to love God's people and recognize His voice. Now he was ready. In Isaiah, chapter 46 and verse 10, God says that unlike us, He "sets the end from the beginning." Like a good movie director shooting the last scene first, then story-boarding each scene toward the grand climactic finish, God prepares and moves us in the direction of our destiny. So all of your life can be training for one specific season and assignment.

(2) I had to sow before I could reap. I sacrificed to get by on half salary or no salary at all, so that our ministry could be built. I tried to be financially responsive to God when it came to my giving, knowing that His Word says, "Be not weary in well

doing: for in due season we shall reap, if we faint not" (Galatians 6:9).

(3) I re-examined the Scriptures. I was raised in a traditional religious culture that viewed success and money as being "worldly." Hence, successful people with money seldom came to our church! As a result we struggled financially. Then God began to show me Scriptures such as, "I am the Lord thy God which teacheth thee to profit, which leadeth thee by the way that thou shouldest go" (Isaiah 48:17). I discovered that not only did God *want* me to succeed, He was actually willing to *show* me how to do it. Then I read Paul's words: "God is able to make all grace abound to you, so that in *all* things at *all* times, having *all* that you need, you will abound in every good work" (2 Corinthians 9:8 NIV). But unless you stand on God's Word and expect His promises to be fulfilled in your life, you'll fail to recognize the strategies He gives you, or to receive His blessings when He sends them your way.

(4) I believe God can trust me. My wife Debby loves to work out in the gym. One day while she was pumping iron she prayed, "Lord, why have you given us an assignment this big?" The Spirit of God within her whispered, "Because I can trust you with it." And He can. We are committed to being good stewards of everything God entrusts to us, making sure it's used for His intended purposes.

Now, I've tried to answer the question, "Bob, why you? And why now?" But the truth is, I don't know. I can think of others who are more qualified. I feel like Moses at the burning bush. I'm saying, "Lord, I didn't start this fire and I can't keep it going. So I'm just going to take off my shoes, acknowledge Your presence, listen to Your voice, obey You, try not to get in Your way, and pray that You will be glorified in everything I do."

Oh, there's one more thing I need to tell you before I finish this chapter: *The greater the assignment, the greater the attack!* Perhaps that's not what you wanted to hear, but it's true. Paul writes, "A great door for effective work has opened to me, and there are many who oppose me" (1Corinthians 16:9 NIV). If you are the recipient of God's blessing—you're a target for the enemy!

And it's not just your enemies you have to watch out for; sometimes the attack comes from those closest to you. Jesus sat at the table with John the beloved on one side and Judas the betrayer on the other. One was close enough to lay his head on Jesus' breast, while the other had sufficient access to betray Him with a kiss. *You need to know who's sitting at your table!*

However, as bad as it is to be attacked by people, it's worse to veer from the course God has charted for you in order to gain their acceptance. As good as it feels to be approved and applauded, at some point you have to stop and ask yourself, "How much am I willing to sacrifice to fulfill my calling?" Your answer will determine your destiny! The Bible says, "Jesus…finished this race…Because he never lost sight of where he was headed…he could put up with anything" (Hebrews 12:2-3 TM). You'll only endure the pain when you've something greater to look forward to.

God exposes you to opposition and criticism in order to strengthen your character; that way when greater blessings (and responsibilities) come, you won't crack. Success comes when you're committed and have a passion to cross the finish line. So the question is, can you handle God's blessing? When the pressure is on will you respond like Nehemiah? "I realized they were plotting to kill me, so I replied by sending back this message to them: I am doing a great work! Why should I stop to come and visit with you?" (Nehemiah 6:2-3 TLB).

To succeed in any worthwhile venture you need "thick skin" when it comes to handling criticism. That's what separates those who *say* they want success from those who are prepared to pay the price for it. For example, if you've been praying for a mate, ask yourself, are you ready for the responsibilities that come with marriage? Are you stable, unselfish and mature enough to provide for a family? Or if you're praying for an increase in your business, are you giving outstanding service to your current clients?

Sometimes we're in love with the *image* of success but we haven't counted the real cost of succeeding. That's why it's a good thing God doesn't automatically give us everything we ask for! God tests you with what you *already* have in order to develop your character and your consistency. He wants to bring you to the place where: (a) You don't cave in under pressure. (b) You learn to love God, the Giver, more than His gifts. And when you get to that place you'll hear Him say, "You are a good...servant...Because you were loyal with small things, I will let you care for much greater things" (Matthew 25:23 NCV).

And that will make it all worthwhile!

CHAPTER SIX

Things to Remember When God Speaks

Jesus told His disciples, "The Spirit...will guide you into all the Truth (the whole, full Truth)" (John 16:13 AMP). Jesus spoke these words to people He'd spent the previous three years with. Now, you'd think if Jesus was with us personally for three years, day and night, we'd have learned all there is to know. But Jesus said to expect more, because He will always have something to say to us about each new situation we are in.

God is interested in the smallest details of your life. Never hesitate to take what you think are small things to Him; after all, *everything* is small to God! He even keeps track of how many hairs you have on your head (See Matthew 10:30). He cares about the desires of your heart (See Psalm 37:4). He wants to reveal truth to you that will set you free from worry and fear (See John 8:32).

God's plan to share an intimate relationship with you existed before you were even born. Paul said that God "determined the times set for them and the exact places where they should live. God did this so that men would seek him" (Acts 17:26-27 NIV). Now if God plans all of our days and where we're going to live before we're even born, then nothing in life should be more important than learning to recognize His voice and be led by Him.

But if you are *unwilling* to listen to God in one area, you'll be *unable* to hear from Him in others. People think they can't hear from God, when in reality there are a lot of things they already know He wants them to do, and they haven't done. The more quickly you do whatever it is the Lord tells you to do, the more quickly He will reveal the next step you are to take.

Hearing from God must be developed by practice—especially if you're a talker! That's why He says: "Be still, and know that I am God" (Psalm 46:10). Our flesh is full of energy and usually wants to be *doing* something, so it can be difficult for us to be still.

You say, "I don't think I've ever heard from God." Could it be that you haven't learned to recognize His voice? When you ask God for something, it's time to listen. Even if He doesn't respond at that moment, He will in due time. You may be doing some ordinary task when He decides to speak to you. But if you've honored Him by listening as part of your fellowship with Him, He'll speak to you at the right time. You need to have an attitude that says, "God, no matter what anyone else is telling me, or what I think or feel, if I hear You saying something to me I'm going to honor You by doing what You say."

If we pray diligently, hear from God, then start asking everybody else what *they* think, we're honoring people's opinion above God's! This will prevent us from developing a relationship in which we consistently hear from Him. We need to *trust* God to instruct us without needing constant reassurance from others. "The anointing (the sacred appointment, the unction) which you received from Him abides [permanently] in you; [so] then you have no need that anyone should instruct you...His anointing teaches you concerning everything and is true...so you must abide in (live in, never depart from) Him" (1 John 2:27 AMP). This verse isn't saying we don't need anybody to teach us God's Word. But it does say we have God's Spirit living inside us to guide and direct our lives. We might occasionally ask somebody for advice, but we need not go constantly to other people. If we are ever going to develop the ability to hear from God and be led by His Spirit, we have to start making our own decisions—and trust the wisdom God has deposited in our heart. The Devil wants us to think we're not capable of hearing from God.

Wrong! The Holy Spirit that dwells inside us will give us confidence, comfort and counsel for our lives. So, we must learn to listen to Him!

But a word of caution: When God speaks to you it's not always wise to rush out and tell people. Doing that can hurt you! When God gives you a word of *direction* it's often followed by a season of *preparation*.

Who wouldn't want to talk about the amazing experience Paul had with God on the Damascus Road? And there would be a "right time" for doing it—but not yet. Why? (a) Because sometimes God needs to go ahead of you and prepare the hearts of those He's sending you to. (b) You need time, maturing and equipping, so that the word you've received can take root within you and be fulfilled in the way God wants.

Paul writes, "Immediately after my calling—without consulting anyone around me and without going up to Jerusalem to confer with those who were apostles long before I was—I got away to

Arabia...it was three years before I went up to Jerusalem to compare stories with Peter...Then I began my ministry" (Galatians 1:16-21 TM).

Paul had the wisdom to know that people would find his calling hard to accept. So he waited. He allowed God to go ahead of him and arrange the circumstances in his favor. And while he was waiting he allowed the word he'd received to grow in his heart and manifest itself in his life. Then, and only then, did he start doing what he was called to do. Paul didn't try to convince anybody; he let God do that. And the result? "[The] response [of others] was to recognize and worship God because of *me*" (Galatians 1:24 TM).

So don't get ahead of God. Be sensitive to His timing!

CHAPTER SEVEN

Not Knowing

The Space Shuttle's guidance system only kicks in when it's several miles up in space. And God's guidance system works the same way. It kicks in when you're in motion, headed in the right direction. But first you've got to get off the launching pad! Are you praying, "Lord, I won't make a move till I hear from You," and He's saying, "You'll get further instructions when you do what I've already told you to do"?

Sometimes we know what God wants but we don't like it, so we pray hoping He'll change His mind and rubber-stamp our desires. We're like the guy who was walking along a cliff ledge and fell over. As he plummeted to his death he noticed a tree limb growing out of the rock face and he grabbed it. But you can't hang on in that position too long. So he shouted, "Help! Is there anybody up there?" A voice said, "Yes, I'm the Lord, trust Me and let go." He thought about it for a moment, then shouted, "Is there anybody *else* up there?"

The Bible says, "By faith Abraham, when called to go to a place he would later receive as his inheritance, obeyed and went, even though he did not know where he was going" (Hebrews 11:8 NIV). When you follow God, you'll go out "not knowing" as much as you'd like to. It's called "faith-walking."

By faith I left Ireland at seventeen, "knowing" in my heart that I'd been called to preach. The door had opened for me to go to America. God provided me with a wonderful mentor in the person of Dr. Gordon Magee, my spiritual father, who at that time was pastoring a church in Houston, Texas.

But I arrived in Houston with two sermons in a briefcase, twenty-five cents in my pocket, no formal training for ministry, "not knowing" how everything would come together. Would anybody invite me to speak? Would I be able to measure up? How would I pay my bills? Yet when I got there God provided everything I needed.

And He did it day by day and step by step!

When Debby and I were invited to go to Romania in 1991 after the fall of the old Ceausescu government, we didn't know what we'd find. We believed this was the one and only time we'd make the trip.

But what we saw in Romania broke our hearts: 250,000 children living (and dying) in state-run institutions, in conditions animals shouldn't be subjected to. Twenty percent of them had contracted AIDS through unprotected blood supplies. Fifty percent had Hepatitis B, and all of them suffered from parasites that lived in the unsanitary water supply.

At first we wept, then we rolled up our sleeves and went to work. We helped organize truck convoys of humanitarian aid to make the five-day journey from Belfast, Ireland, where Debby and I were born, to seventy-two of Romania and Moldova's worst orphanages.

Forty-seven trips later we had helped to build not one, but two transitional homes for orphaned and abandoned children called *The Village of Hope.* Since then we've rescued hundreds of children, rehabilitated and resocialized them, and placed them into foster families. Each month we support many of these families. When the U.S. Ambassador to Romania visited *The Village of Hope,* the Child Protection Services told him, "It's a model home for the rest of the country."

And we couldn't have done it alone. When God calls you to do a job, He calls others to stand with you. So special thanks to my partners around the world, also to my friend Ian Mackie who heads up United Christian Broadcasters in the U.K. and Ireland, and to the supporters of that wonderful ministry which is impacting the nations of Europe for Christ.

When you follow God you "go out not knowing," as much as you'd like to, and He informs you on an "as need to know" basis.

As a teen growing up in Belfast, I rode my bike to work, to church, and everywhere else. We were dirt-poor and it was my only means of transportation. It was also good exercise, liberated me from the tyranny of bus schedules, and best of all, required no fuel or insurance premiums. The thing I remember about that bike is, its small headlight never shone more than a few feet ahead. Are you getting the idea? That's how God guides us—a few feet at a time!

Abraham "obeyed and went, even though he did not know where he was going." He wasn't given a flow chart or a road map, just a command to leave where he was and head toward Canaan. Later God gave him very specific direction, but only when he was in motion and had obeyed what God had already told him to do.

Abraham didn't know where he was going— but he knew he had to leave where he was! If all you know is that you can't stay where you are, that's enough to create movement in the right direction.

"On the third day Abraham looked up and saw the place in the distance" (Genesis 22:4 NIV). If you had asked Abraham during the first two days of his journey what his destination would look like, he couldn't have told you. He only knew that he was following God's instructions.

And what happened when he got there? "Abraham looked up and there in a thicket he saw a ram caught by its horns" (Genesis 22:13 NIV). God stretched Abraham's faith to the limits. Only when he was ready to plunge a dagger into the heart of his beloved son Isaac, did God say "stop." Did God want a human sacrifice? No, He just wanted to know if there was *anything* Abraham loved more than Him. Abraham proved there wasn't, so God knew that there was no level of blessing He couldn't entrust to him.

Notice also that the ram was "caught by its

horns." It wanted to escape, but it couldn't. It was held securely in place until Abraham arrived. Understand this: *nobody* can take what God has prepared for you. You don't need to pursue certain individuals thinking they hold the key to your future. Nor do you have to worry, or try to manipulate the circumstances to your advantage. While Abraham was climbing one side of the mountain the ram was climbing the other, and God arranged a meeting at the top. That's why Abraham called the name of this special place "Jehovah Jireh," which means "The Lord will Provide" (Genesis 22:14 NIV).

The truth is, if you depend on certain people too long you can end up under a "spirit of obligation." Yes, they'll make you feel indebted to them, and that can be dangerous. God uses people as His *instruments,* but He alone is the *source* of all you need. People will enter your life and people will leave. So bless them when they come and bless them when they go, and remind yourself that if the Lord provided for you before, He'll do it again—

and keep moving forward.

If you were fortunate enough to receive a large check in the mail, hopefully you wouldn't fall in love with the mailman, invite him to dinner or try to strike up a long-term relationship. No, he's just the carrier of your blessing. He doesn't even know what's in the envelope. It came from a different source. Are you getting the point? God alone is your source; where He guides, He provides!

But there's another way in which God guides us—by closing the door. And that can be difficult for us. Instead of green, all our lights are now red. What's God up to?

In Acts, chapter 16, we read about Paul on one of his missionary journeys. "Paul and his companions traveled throughout the region of Phrygia and Galatia, having been kept by the Holy Spirit from preaching the word in the province of Asia. When they came to the border of Mysia, they tried to enter Bithynia, but the Spirit of Jesus would not allow them to. So they passed by Mysia and went down to Troas. During the night Paul had a vision of a man of Macedonia standing and begging him, 'Come over to Macedonia and help us.' After Paul had seen the vision, we got ready at once to leave for Macedonia, concluding that God had called us to preach the gospel to them" (Acts 16:6-10 NIV).

Pastor Paul Scanlon points out that the Apostle Paul's mentality was that everywhere was an option, everywhere was a potential "yes" until God said "no." Paul simply pointed his life in the general direction of the great commission, "Go into all the world." And only when Paul was in motion did God guide him by both prevention and permission. When God prevented Paul from entering Asia and Bithynia, he didn't stay there praying about *why* God prohibited him, he just kept moving. For Paul, trying something and it not working out was no big deal. He lived believing that his gift to God was his mobility, and God's gift to him was that He would always guide him to where he needed to be. The way God guided Paul's life in Acts 16 could be called "guidance by prohibition," or guidance by what God doesn't allow. This form of Divine guidance is perhaps the least understood and is therefore the most difficult for us to understand or accept. What God denies and keeps us away from, is as much Divine guidance as what He permits and opens up to us. Every door that didn't open, every opportunity you didn't get and every call that didn't come, is as much God's guidance as those that did.

As you begin to mature in your walk with God, you look back and thank Him for two things: (1) the grace to accept closed doors; (2) the faith to walk through open ones!

CHAPTER EIGHT

What Have We Learned?

So, what have we learned thus far? We've learned that God leads us through the people He puts in our lives, through the voice of His indwelling Spirit, through wise leadership, through open and closed doors, through unmet needs, through the desires and skill-sets He's placed within us, and through our listening spiritual ear. Yes. "A man's steps are directed by the Lord" (Proverbs 20:24 NIV).

But once you begin to recognize God's voice and be led by Him, what then? How do you stay on the path? What must you always keep in mind?

That's what the rest of this book is about.

CHAPTER NINE

Think Outside the Box

Have you heard about the frog that was born at the bottom of a well? He thought life couldn't get any better until one day he looked up and saw daylight. Climbing up to investigate, he was amazed to find a much larger pond than the one he lived in. And going further afield, he discovered a lake that was bigger again. When eventually he came to the ocean and all he could see was water, it dawned on him just how limited his thinking had been. He thought everything he needed was down in the well, but that was a drop in the bucket compared to the things God had out there for him to enjoy.

Are you living today in your own little "well,"

reluctant to leave your comfort zone, settling for a limited and safe existence?

In Ezekiel, chapter 47, God shows the prophet a river that flowed from His presence, blessing everything it touched. But it started small. First it was ankle deep (See Ezekiel 47:3 NIV), then it was knee deep (See Ezekiel 47:4 NIV), then it was waist deep (See Ezekiel 47:4 NIV), then it became a river "deep enough to swim in" (See Ezekiel 47:5 NIV). God has rivers of blessing, deep enough to swim in. Wouldn't you like to step out in faith, experience new depths in Him and go where you've never been before?

Remember, the enemy will do everything he can to keep you focused on your background, your lack of education, your appearance, and your limited resources. Bruce Wilkinson says, "It doesn't matter whether you're short of money, people, energy, or time, what God invites you to do will always be greater than the resources you start with." You don't have to let fear limit your vision when God is your source, because His supply is unlimited! One idea from Him, just one, can change your entire life and the lives of others.

God has great things in store for you—so start thinking outside the box!

CHAPTER TEN

Be Persistent

Nehemiah wept over the broken-down walls of Jerusalem, the city he loved. Then he went to work rebuilding them. And it wasn't easy. His enemies threatened him day and night. His construction crews built the walls with a trowel in one hand and a sword in the other. Building and battling—they always go together. Against all odds, fifty-two days later they stowed their gear and walked away from a newly completed wall. How did they do it? The record reads, "So built we the wall...for the people had a mind to work" (Nehemiah 4:6).

The will of God is a battlefield, not a bed of roses. Paul writes, "We are pressed on every side by troubles, but not crushed and broken. We are perplexed because we don't know why things happen as they do, but we don't give up and quit. We are hunted down, but God never abandons us. We get knocked down, but we get up again and keep going" (2 Corinthians 4:8-9 TLB). It's no surprise that Paul changed the world he lived in. He was relentless!

One day in 1947, Lester Wunderman was arbitrarily fired from his advertising job in New York. But he felt that he still had a lot to learn from the head of the agency, Max Sackheim. So next morning Wunderman went back to his office and began working just as he had before. He talked to co-workers and clients; he sat in on meetings—all without pay. Sackheim ignored him for a month. Finally he walked up to Wunderman. "OK, you win," he said, shaking his head. "I never saw a man who wanted a job more than he wanted money."

That kind of persistence paid off for Wunderman. He went on to become one of the most successful advertising men of the century, and is known as the father of direct marketing. He's credited with having invented preprinted news-paper inserts, bound-in subscription cards for magazines and subscription cards such as those used by Time-Life Books and the Columbia Record Club.

Now, advertising may not be your thing—but action must be. What are you willing to do to achieve your God-given dream? Work without pay like Lester Wunderman? Endure criticism and threats like Nehemiah? Keep getting back up like Paul? Success begins at the beginning, and con-tinues with consistent action.

Take a moment and consider the following six thoughts by Dr. John Maxwell: (1) You don't have to be great to start, but you do have to start to be great. (2) The first two letters in the word goal are GO. (3) Some people dream of worthy accom-plishments, while others wake up and do them. (4) Anybody who brags about what he's going to do tomorrow, probably did the same thing yesterday. (5) You'll never be what you ought to be, until you're first doing what you ought to be doing. (6) If you have trouble thinking outside the box, you're probably in the wrong box. Get out of there!

CHAPTER ELEVEN

Be Humble

A newly-elected member of the British Parliament took his eight-year-old daughter on a brief tour of London. When they came to Westminster Abbey the awesomeness of it struck the little girl. She stood looking up at the towering columns, studying their beauty and grandeur. Her father, intrigued at her concentration, looked down and said, "Sweetheart, what are you thinking about?" She said "Daddy, I was thinking how big you seem at home, and how small you look in here."

God's presence has a way of humbling us. And that's good, because only when we empty ourselves of pride, does God have a vessel He can use.

Your Bible overflows with examples of those

who did this. In his Gospel, Matthew mentions his own name only twice. Both times he calls himself a tax-collector, a despised profession. In his list of apostles, he assigns himself the eighth spot. John doesn't even mention his name in his Gospel. The twenty appearances of the name "John" all refer to the Baptist. John the Apostle simply calls himself "the other disciple," or "the disciple whom Jesus loved." Luke wrote two of the most important books in the Bible, but never once penned his own name. Paul, the Bible's most prolific author, referred to himself as "a fool" (2 Corinthians 12:11). He also called himself "the least of the apostles" (1 Corinthians 15:9). Five years later he claimed to be "less than the least of all saints" (Ephesians 3:8). In one of his final epistles he referred to himself as "the chief of sinners" (see 1 Timothy 1:15). As Paul grew older his ego grew smaller. King David wrote no psalm celebrating his victory over Goliath. But he wrote a public poem of repentance confessing his sin with Bathsheba.

Why is humility so important? Because God "guides the humble in what is right and teaches them his way" (Psalm 25:9 NIV).

Peter writes, "All of you, clothe yourselves with humility...for God is opposed to the proud, but gives grace to the humble. Therefore humble yourselves under the mighty hand of God, that He may exalt you at the proper time, casting all your anxiety on Him, because He cares for you" (1 Peter 5:5-7 NAS). Peter expressed four very important thoughts here. And he combined them for a reason. Let's look at each:

(1) "All of you, clothe yourselves with humility toward one another." Peter's expression "clothe yourselves with humility" may have referred to a white scarf or apron typically worn by servants. We're called to be servants, not celebrities! "All" lets us know we stand on an equal footing before the cross, daily in need of God's enabling grace.

(2) "God is opposed to the proud, but gives grace to the humble." When you are ego-driven,

you're at odds with God, but when you remain humble you enjoy His richest blessings.

(3) "Humble yourselves under the mighty hand of God, that He may exalt you at the proper time." The phrase "the mighty hand of God" is used in Scripture to symbolize two things: God's hand of discipline and His hand of deliverance. And you need both.

(4) "Casting all your anxiety on Him, because He cares for you." Peter addresses the core issue: worry that if we don't watch out for ourselves, nobody else will. But if we believe that God "cares for us," we needn't worry about serving our own interests. We can focus on the needs of others, confident that God will spare nothing when it comes to meeting *our* needs.

Dr. Paul Brand was one of the 20th Century's most respected physicians because of his work amongst lepers. His love for India's "least of the least" led him to pioneer surgical techniques which surgeons still use today in orthopedic reconstruction. He was a brilliant physician, medical teacher, writer, speaker, and champion for the underdog.

Philip Yancey writes: "Meeting Dr. Brand, I realized I had misconstrued humility as a negative self-image. Paul Brand obviously knew his gifts: he had finished first throughout his academic career and had attended many awards banquets honoring his accomplishments. Yet he recognized his gifts as just that, *gifts* from a loving Creator, and he used them in a Christ-like way of service. When I first met him Brand was still adjusting to life in the United States. Everyday luxuries made him nervous and he longed for a simple life close to the soil. He knew presidents, kings and celebrities, yet he rarely mentioned them. He talked openly about his failures and always deflected credit for his successes to his associates. Most impressive to me, the wisest and most brilliant man I have ever met, devoted much of his life to some of the lowliest people on the planet."

Genuinely humble people always seek the

well-being of others. And they are very secure. They're aware of their gifts and the attributes that make them successful at whatever they do. And that security—that honest, healthy self-assessment—results in more than a humble attitude: one that translates into actions which can be observed, actions which make a difference, and a lifestyle we should want to follow.

CHAPTER TWELVE

Do It Now!

The most dangerous word in the dictionary is "someday."

We spend our whole lives waiting for someday: someday when I graduate, someday when I get a job, someday when I get married, someday when we have kids, someday when I retire. Dale Carnegie writes, "One of the most tragic things I know about human nature is that all of us tend to put off living. We are all dreaming of some magical rose garden over the horizon—instead of enjoying the roses that are blooming outside our windows today."

Start living now. Seize each moment. The big, obviously dramatic ones, and the small, apparently insignificant ones—every moment is precious;

every one is God's gift to you and you must learn to live in it.

The biggest problem with the "someday syndrome" is that it robs you of living right now. You don't hear God's voice in this moment, and as a result you never become what God intends you to be. Procrastinating is ultimately a subtle way of saying "no" to what God is calling you to do.

"What can I do to change?" you ask.

(1) Stop procrastinating! Rise up and say, "I'm taking responsibility for my life. It's not up to somebody else, it's up to me. The ball is in my court."

(2) Take action. Think of one task you've been putting off. Divide it up into small steps and take the first step today—before you go to bed tonight! Motivation follows action. If you wait to do something until you feel like it, it won't happen. Take an action step, and you'll find yourself becoming energized.

(3) Prioritize your life. Decide what's important and what is not. Live—so that if somebody

just looks at the way you live, they'll know what really matters to you.

(4) Understand that your life is short. You will be eternally alive, but your life on earth is brief. The Psalmist writes, "Teach us to number our days aright, that we may gain a heart of wisdom" (Psalm 90:12 NIV). Ask God to help you prioritize your days. Don't let a single one of them slip away!

CHAPTER THIRTEEN

Eliminate Hurry

Are you too busy to read your Bible, to pray, or to pause and get God's input? Do you set your own goals, then ask Him to help you reach them? Do you devise your own plans and ask Him to bless them? How long have you been living like this? How many times have you promised yourself to do better? Do you think it'll just "happen" some day? Not a chance!

John Ortberg writes, "When I first moved to Chicago I called a friend of mine—the wisest spiritual man I know—and asked him, 'What do I need to do to be healthy spiritually?' There was a long pause. Then he said, 'You must ruthlessly eliminate hurry from your life.' There was another long pause, and finally I said, 'OK. I wrote that one down. Now, what *else* do you have to tell me, because I don't have much time and I want to get a lot of wisdom out of this conversation.' He replied, 'There is nothing else. Hurry is the great enemy of spiritual life in our day. It has had other enemies in other days, but in our day hurry is the great enemy of spiritual life because you can hardly do anything the way Jesus did it if you are in a hurry. You cannot love in a hurry. You cannot listen to a child in a hurry. Jesus was often busy. But there's an important distinction between hurry and busy. Busy is an external condition—a condition of the body. Jesus was often busy but He was never hurried. Hurried is an inward condition in which you are so frantic and preoccupied that you are unable to receive love from the father, unable to be present with other people, or to give them love.'"

Understand this: things will not just "settle down" in your life. If you wait "to get around" to what really matters, you'll never do what God's called you to do or become what He meant you to be. Your soul will wither. You must ruthlessly eliminate hurry from your life.

And no one else can do this for you—not your boss, or your pastor, or your spouse, or your kids, or your best friend. No, you must do this for yourself.

Take a moment and think about these two Scriptures: (1) "The fear [reverence and acknowledgement] of the Lord leads to life: Then one rests content, untouched by trouble" (Proverbs 19:23 NIV). (2) "Desire without knowledge is not good, and one who moves too hurriedly misses the way" (Proverbs 19:2 NRSV).

CHAPTER FOURTEEN

Focus on Your Strengths

Here's a rule of thumb for success: "Work where you're strongest eighty percent of the time. Work where you're learning fifteen percent of the time. Work where you're weakest five percent of the time."

Is that scriptural? Absolutely! "If your gift is that of serving others, serve them well. If you are a teacher, do a good job of teaching. If you are a preacher, see to it that your sermons are strong and helpful. If God has given you money, be generous in helping others with it. If God has given you administrative ability and put you in charge of the work of others, take the responsibility seriously" (Romans 12:7-8 TLB).

What happens to a team when its members constantly play "out of position?" First, morale deteriorates because the team isn't playing up to its capacity. Then resentment sets in; those working in an area of weakness resent that their best is untapped. And others on the team who know that they could better fill a mismatched position are upset that their skills are being overlooked. Before long they become unwilling to work as a team. Then everyone's confidence erodes and the situation keeps getting worse. The team stops progressing and the competition takes advantage of their weakness. As a result, they never win.

When people aren't positioned where they do things well, things don't run well. Do you know what your greatest strengths are? If not, follow these guidelines:

(1) *Be secure:* If you allow your insecurities to get the better of you, you'll become inflexible and resistant to change. And if you can't change you won't grow. (2) *Get to know yourself:* Spend time

reflecting on and exploring your gifts. Acknowledge your blind spots. Ask others for feedback.
(3) Trust your leader: If you can't trust your
leader—join another team. *(4) See the big picture:*
Your place on any team makes sense only in the
context of the big picture. If your only motivation
for finding your niche is personal gain, your wrong
motives will rob you of the fulfillment and success
you desire. *(5) Learn from experience:* There's only
one way to know you've discovered your niche—
take risks, try things, learn from your mistakes. A
great man was once asked the secret of his success.
He replied, "By making good decisions." The ques-
tioner then asked, "How did you learn to make
good decisions?" The great man smiled and
replied, "By making bad ones!"

Edgar W. Work said, "The real tragedy of life is
not in being limited to one talent, but in the failure
to use that one talent." If you want to make the
most of your life do these three things:

(a) Maximize what God has given you. Thomas

Edison set himself an ambitious goal: to come up with a major new invention every six months, and a minor one every ten days. When he died he held 1,093 U.S. patents, and more than 2,000 foreign ones. He made his dreams a reality by sticking to what he did best. Thomas Wolf wrote, "If a man has a talent and doesn't use it, he has failed. If he has a talent and uses only half of it, he has partly failed. If he has a talent and learns somehow to use the whole of it, he has gloriously succeeded and won a satisfaction and a triumph few men will ever know."

(b) *Start where you are.* After striking out in a baseball game, cartoon character Charlie Brown pours out his heart to his friend Lucy: "All my life I've dreamed of pitching in the big leagues, but I know I'll never make it!" Lucy replies, "You're thinking too far ahead, Charlie Brown. What you need to do is set yourself more immediate goals. Start with the next inning, for example. When you go out to pitch, see if you can walk to the mound…

without falling down." Success starts with the first step. Exercise your faith and take that step.

(c) Focus on the "one thing" God has called you to do. Music was everything to Brahms. He collected music and studied compositions going back to the fifteenth century. He worked feverishly to perfect his craft, refusing to publish anything that didn't meet his exacting standards. That is why he didn't publish his first symphony until he was forty years old, and never married, saying it would distract him from his vocation. "I am in love with music" he once wrote, "I think of nothing but, and of other things only when they make music more beautiful."

Is that fanaticism? No, it's focus, and it's what makes your life count!

CHAPTER FIFTEEN

Live in God's Presence

The Psalmist said, "I have set the Lord always before me" (Psalm 16:8). We must learn to recognize God's presence in our *minds*, our *thoughts* and our *feelings*. We must learn to continually focus our attention on Him, to think about Him, talk to Him often, ask for His help, tell Him our plans, pour out our heart to Him, describe our problems, listen carefully to His voice, and give thanks for His joy.

The words, "I have set the Lord always before me," are the key to recognizing God's voice and being led by Him. When certain thoughts are present, there's a good chance that they are the result of God's walking alongside us. For example:

The first thought you'll have when God is present, is a sense of *reassurance*. Whatever you do in life, God longs to partner with you. Whether it's Joshua facing the challenge of taking over from Moses and leading the nation, or Paul at sea, going through the worst storm of his life, the message is always the same: "Be not afraid. I am with you."

The second thought you'll have when God is present, is that you'll get *guidance*. Maybe you're stumped by some issue, then an idea comes to you. It might be a big idea or a small one, but it will help. Or you're with someone and you're about to say something stupid, something self-promotional, something that will inflict damage. All of a sudden a little voice within says, "Be quiet." Where does that voice come from? It comes from God. And every time you listen and respond you increase your capacity for being with God, and it's a little more likely that you'll become the kind of person He can use.

A third indicator of God's presence is *conviction*

of sin. You're going down the wrong road and a little stab of pain says, "No, turn around." Learn to heed that voice or you'll lose your way, forfeit God's blessing, violate your values, diminish your influence with others, and end up guilt-ridden and defeated.

The fourth kind of thought that will tell you God is present is *joy.* You can't walk with God without His joy spilling over into your life. "[O Lord], you have made known to me the path of life; you will fill me with joy in your presence" (Psalm 16:11 NIV). It works like this: you put in an extra effort, something gets accomplished and you feel a surge of satisfaction—that's what happened when God was creating the world and He said, "That's good!" When that happens, God is closer than you think.

God can use any of these things to convey His presence. If you "Set the Lord always before you" you'll begin to recognize His voice and sense His leadings in your ordinary, everyday life.

What could be better than that?

Acknowledgments

Come Before Winter and Share My Hope
Charles R. Swindoll/Living Books

**Cure for the Common Life:
Living in Your Sweet Spot**
Max Lucado/W. Publishing

Your Best Life Now
Joel Osteen/Warner Faith

**The Ten Commandments of
Working in a Hostile Environment**
T.D. Jakes/Berkley Books

Talent Is Never Enough
John C. Maxwell/Thomas Nelson

God Is Closer Than You Think
John Ortberg/Zondervan

Perfect Trust
Charles R. Swindoll/J. Countryman

Today Matters
John C. Maxwell/Warner Faith

The Finishing Touch
Charles R. Swindoll/Word Publishing

Life Essentials
Tony Evans/Moody Publishers

Woman to Woman:
Candid Conversations from Me to You
Joyce Meyer/Time Warner Book Group

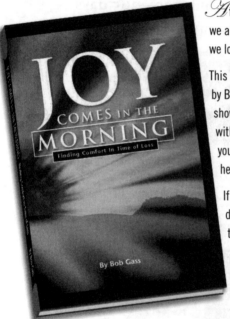

To find more books, CD's
and videos by the author,
visit **www.bobgass.com** today.